THE MARA MINDSHIFT GUIDE

Praise for
THE MARA MINDSHIFT GUIDE

"This is Fantastic! Easy to understand and applicable to anyone. I think even people who aren't trading should read this. I love the exercises, and the way the book also takes you alongside Bob as a real-world example. Well done!"

- Austin Silver, Co-Owner,
Head of Trading & Education at ASFX

"I really liked the workbook questions. Kept me engaged and wanting to progress to the next one."

- Akil Stokes,
Co-Founder of Tier One Trading

"I wouldn't change a thing! Very very very well done."
- Adam Sarhan, CEO 50 Park

"I love it! Especially the 'cutting cord' bit at the end. I also love the weed analogy!"

- Jason Graystone,
Co-Founder of Tier-One Trading

"I went through the workbook and it's solid. This should help people improve their trading and mindset."

- Rizwan Memon-
Founder & President of Riz International

THE MARA MINDSHIFT GUIDE

A TRADING BELIEFS WORKBOOK

MICHAEL LAMOTHE

"What if we are exactly where we are supposed to be? What if the things we have gone through are the lessons we are supposed to learn to serve something else? Then isn't it our duty to do something bigger?"

– Michael Lamothe

CONTENTS

INTRODUCTION

Hi! I'm Mike Lamothe, the founder of MARA. Our goal is to help individuals like you succeed in the market by overcoming the single biggest hurdle all traders face… Mindset.

When I first started trading, I made every mistake in the book. In fact, sometimes I think the reason I finally started winning is because I ran out of ways to lose!

But in all seriousness, I finally started to come out ahead once I:

a)   Realized my mindset was broken and in desperate need of repair.
b)   Got off my behind and did something about it.

Ideas without action have no real value. They're kinda like that trade you saw but never took.

Conversely, action without a plan is like the trade you may have taken on a hot tip and then had no idea how to manage it.

By doing the exercises in this MARA Mindshift Guide you will be doing both following a plan and taking real action. This isn't a quick fix. This will require you to take a hard look in the mirror, no easy task for anyone. Few follow through with it…and few have lasting results. However, cultivating awareness of your beliefs and working to rise them will be a game changer for your trading and your life! This beliefs guide will serve as a roadmap for you to manage your mindset and get you on the path to trading victory.

In trading it can feel like a mad rush to the finish line. And many people end up with their account dying before they even get past mile one. There's a lot more to trading than clicking "buy" or "sell", just like there's a lot more to running a marathon than putting one foot in front of the other. It is training (ideally with a coach and a team), having the tools you need to get through the walls you'll be confronted with in the race toward the finish line, and most importantly—a mindset of steel.

When I had my first taste of the market back in 1998, I knew none of this and it took me a decade to finally become a consistently profitable trader. No one should have to struggle for that long!

My goal is to help you avoid countless years of needless struggle by helping you:

1. Gain awareness of your beliefs.
2. Achieve clarity on your goals.
3. Identify which beliefs are helping you achieve your goals and which are holding you back.

4. Remove the beliefs that aren't serving you.
5. Install beliefs that do serve you.

My sincerest hope is that you become better prepared, have far greater success, and have an easier time achieving it all than I did. I believe that giving your full effort to the exercises in this workbook will help you get there.

Millions prepare for this trading race without giving a second thought to mindset. They struggle and fail over and over again.

But you are taking real action today! You are taking charge and setting out to do the essential work to rise above the fray and prepare yourself for something greater.

· · · · · · · ● · · · · · · · ·

What would happen to your trading if you were increasingly aware of your beliefs?

Unfortunately, most people aren't aware. Most choose to remain oblivious and end up limiting themselves in the process. They either don't want to deal with the pain of letting go, are fearful about what happens if they do, or perhaps a little of both.

HERE'S A QUICK STORY:

A client of mine named Bob was a trader and a bodybuilder. He worshiped his dad. Even though they didn't have much, Bob and his two younger brothers always had enough. Their dad worked 3 jobs to make it happen.

His father would say things like, "Nothing comes easy Bob. If you want something, you need to work hard for it. Hard work pays son."

Bob would hear stuff like this all the time from his old man. It inspired him. It helped him win body building competitions. **But unfortunately, Bob applied this belief in a way that tripped up his trading.**

He would work hard. Spend hours in front of the charts, reading books, taking courses. He'd make progress. But as soon as things felt like they were getting easier, Bob would give back every last penny he made! Why?

Well, if Bob wanted the answer and to make it as a trader, he'd need to start questioning his beliefs. Together, he and I started digging deeper. Beliefs are like car batteries and some can have a really strong charge to them.

You are the sole driver of this 'beliefs car'. For better or worse, all the beliefs in it remain charged unless YOU do something about it.

Through our discourse, I discovered that Bob's beliefs about hard work were not helping his trading. They were actually holding him back! He believed that he had to work hard for money. Not only that, if it came easily, he wasn't worthy of it.

Now if I had simply told Bob flat out that this belief was the thing holding him back it likely would have put him on the defensive. It helped him in other areas of his life. Why not trading?? He had to come to this conclusion himself.

To help Bob come to this realization on his own, I asked him a few questions about his body building. He fondly told me about his most recent feat. Deadlifting 400 kilos!

"Damn! That's impressive!" I said when he told me. "Was it easy for you?"

"No," Bob said. "I can lift that amount for only one rep."

"How much were you able to lift last year?"

"Last year I could only do 300, I've come a long way, right?"

"Wow, you sure have! That's massive progress in only a year! Congrats! How hard is it for you to lift those 300 kilos now?"

"Easy! I can practically warm up with that amount now."

Bob didn't know it but I was about to compare his lifting to trading. I asked a very weird question "So are you no longer worthy of lifting 300 kilos?"

"What??" Bob was baffled by my question. "Of course I'm worthy! I worked hard to get here. And that's not stoppin' anytime soon!"

And then I asked him the following question:

"Couldn't the same be said of your trading? You worked hard and it got easier. Aren't you worthy of the ease now because you've put in the work?"

A light bulb turned on in Bob's head that was so bright you could see it from space! He had a major breakthrough– realizing his beliefs about hard work and money were holding him back.

Over time and by continuing to work together through my coaching service, Bob's trading immensely improved. He shed major limiting beliefs, became increasingly aware of his trading beliefs, and was trading in line with beliefs that would serve him well and lead him closer to his goals.

And this is why having *Awareness of your Beliefs will be a Game Changer to your trading!*

We will discuss this and so much more in this Mindshift Guide. Your trading is about to take a quantum leap forward!

In this Mindshift Guide we will cover 5 Key Mindset Hacks. They are:

1) Know Thyself and Your Beliefs
2) Uncover Your Trading Beliefs
3) Examine Your Money Beliefs
4) Weeding Your Mind of Poor Beliefs
5) Cutting the Cord on Limiting Beliefs

We will also walk through the next steps to installing beliefs and skills that will lead you toward trading mastery.

Today you are taking the first step, just like Bob did, to become more aware of your beliefs and to realize if they are helping or hurting your trading. It is only through AWARENESS that you can begin the process. That awareness starts today.

This workbook is filled with exercises to help guide you through this process. Please take the time to fill out the answers! These exercises are meant to be spaced apart so that you give yourself time to contemplate the questions and your answers to them.

Congrats on taking this Journey! Remember, you are not alone. I am with you every step of the way!

LET'S GET STARTED WITH THE FIVE KEY MINDSET HACKS!

HACK #1

'Know Thyself' and Your Beliefs

We have beliefs about everything. These beliefs guide our actions. And since they guide our actions, they literally dictate our performance in the market. A trader's beliefs decide whether she or he succeeds or fails. Period. So, isn't it critical then to become increasingly aware of what our beliefs really are?

Unfortunately most traders aren't aware. And so they continue to fail. I failed for close to a decade before realizing any of this.

Our beliefs are made up of what we've seen, heard, and were taught since birth. They were all useful to us at some point. But it's up to us to figure out if they still are.

Do you remember what it was like when you first learned about Santa Claus? How it felt finding presents under the tree?

How about when you finally learned there was no Santa Claus? How did you feel then?

Beliefs can often be painful to let go of whether they're serving us or not. When it's painful, what happens?

Well... a few things.

Suppose you're grinding away day and night trying to learn trading. Reading books. Watching videos. Maybe even buying a course or getting a mentor.

You understand a lot about trading but for some reason, every time you start making some progress, WHAM! You feel like you're back to square one.

THIS EVER HAPPEN TO YOU?

What if you grew up watching your parents argue about money?

How about if you were told there was never enough of it? That the things you wanted growing up, you couldn't have because money was tight and hard to come by?

What if you were told that money corrupts? That it's the root of all evil? That having too much of it was a bad thing?

What if you heard things like this as a child? Could they still be living somewhere in your subconscious as an adult? And if so, would you necessarily be aware of it?

What would happen to *your* trading if *you* were increasingly aware of *your* beliefs?

In order to become a successful trader, **you need to become increasingly aware of your beliefs.**

The following exercise will help jumpstart this process for you.

EXERCISE #1A:
WHY ARE YOU TRADING?

Why are you trading? What are you hoping to achieve by doing it?

Is Trading fun for you? Why or Why not?

On a fun scale of 1-10, how would you rate it?

EXERCISE #1A:
WHY ARE YOU TRADING?

If you gave trading a 'fun score' of 6 or less, ask yourself if trading really is your thing?

Give it some thought. It's okay if it's not. You can still profit from the market. Get some of the basics down. Become knowledgeable enough to play in a simple way. Maybe hire the right person to do it for you.

You shouldn't feel like you *have to* trade to achieve your dreams. Life is short and we shouldn't spend significant time doing things we don't enjoy or aren't fun for us.

Now if trading is fun for you, if it is your game, your next step is to get super clear on your WHY. The clearer your why, the more heavy lifting it will do for you.

There's a lot involved in becoming a successful trader. Some of it you may find challenging. A clear and powerful "WHY" will carry you far.

This next exercise will help you peel back the layers to reveal the deeper reasons and more powerful 'whys' behind why trading is important to you.

EXERCISE #1B:
DIGGING INTO YOUR 'WHY'

Why is trading important to you? (Restate your answer from the earlier page). (layer 1)

Why is that important to you? (layer 2)

Why is that important to you? (layer 3)

Why is that important to you? (layer 4)

Why is that important to you? (layer 5)

HACK #1: RECAP

Awesome! You've got a clear and compelling reason for why you're trading!

Keep this with you and read it daily as a reminder. When things get challenging, and they will at times, this will help keep you focused, motivated, and on track.

In completing this exercise you're already WAY AHEAD of most other people learning to trade. Pat yourself on the back. Get up. Stretch. Grab a drink of water. Get energized!

We're about to start tackling your trading beliefs.

HACK #2

Uncover Your
Trading Beliefs

Joe was a guy in his thirties who came to me for some trading advice. He was trading for a few years, blew up multiple accounts, and nothing seemed to be working for him.

Each morning he'd roll out of bed and hit the charts, trying to find his next trade. He looked at charts day and night. He believed that if he put in ample time with the charts then it would give him a 6th sense about market direction and what would happen next.

Unfortunately, whenever Joe was right, it would be AFTER he had already sold for a loss. Frustrated, Joe told himself that all he had to do was hold on longer. And he did. Sometimes this strategy would work and he'd make huge profits. Inevitably, however, holding on for too long also led to some major losses and Joe found himself in a deep hole.

Joe thought he was doing everything traders were supposed to do. Not only was he hitting the charts day and night but he bought a top-of-the-line trading PC with eight screens, and signed up for alerts services. He felt he was really giving it his all to make something happen. But every time he tried to "make something happen" he took one step forward and two steps back.

Joe reached out to me after he had blown up his account for a third time. He was confused. If he had all the right equipment, alert services, and knowledge of the charts, why wasn't he winning? Exasperated, Joe asked me, *"What am I doing wrong? I've tried everything. Why am I failing at trading?"*

I've heard stories like this a thousand times. Feeling like you 'know what to do', you see others doing it, but you still struggle. No one should have to suffer like this along their trading journey.

Joe had a dream of being his own boss, trading from home, and not having to answer to anyone. But he had several limiting beliefs preventing him from achieving his dream.

A big one that he and most others miss is confusing 'not having to answer to anyone' with answering to himself and following a clearly defined trading plan.

Another limiting belief Joe had was about analysis and trade selection leading to riches. Sure, analysis is important, but its only one part of the game. There's a lot more to becoming consistently profitable in the market than analyzing trades.

Unchecked, unquestioned, or unaware, limiting beliefs cause traders to struggle for years while blowing up their accounts again and again.

Joe needed to do some digging. What beliefs does he have about trading? What other beliefs might he unearth and discover are holding him back?

EXERCISE #2A:
UNCOVER YOUR TRADING BELIEFS

You're about to write your beliefs about trading. Write whatever comes to mind. Let it be a stream of consciousness.

Do not judge these beliefs as they come out. That part will come later.

For now, just focus on getting them out of your head and onto the page.

Some examples of beliefs to help get you started:

- "The whole market is rigged."
- "I need to know what the president is going to Tweet next if I want to win."
- "If I follow a proven system, I can become rich from trading."
- "I should risk no more than 1% of capital per trade."

Write Your Answers in the space below and on the next 2 pages. I suggest using bullets or numbers to make it easier to review later

EXERCISE #2A:
UNCOVER YOUR TRADING BELIEFS

Please use this page to continue writing answers to Exercise #2A

EXERCISE #2A:
UNCOVER YOUR TRADING BELIEFS

Please use this page to continue writing answers to Exercise #2A

HACK #2: RECAP

WELL DONE! You are absolutely crushing it so far!

The first time I did that exercise I felt exhausted when I was done.

I recommend taking at least a 5 to 10 minute break before continuing. Keeping your energy high is a great habit to cultivate. It's one I picked up from Brendon Burchard, one of the top leadership coaches in the world!

So give yourself another pat on the back. Get up. Stretch. Grab a drink of water. Get re-energized!

Next up, we're talking money beliefs!

HACK #3

Examine Your
Money Beliefs

Could limiting beliefs about money be the weeds preventing your money tree from growing? **Damn straight they could!**

What if you grew up watching your parents argue about money? How about if you were told there was never enough of it? That the things you wanted growing up, you couldn't have because money was tight. What beliefs about money would you likely have as an adult?

How about if you were told money is the root of all evil? That it corrupts?

Maybe a character in one of your favorite shows had these beliefs? The things you picked up on as a kid may still be living in your subconscious as an adult.

Remember Bob, the bodybuilder, from earlier in this workbook? Bob's money beliefs stemmed from his childhood. He thought he needed to work hard for money. Not only that, if it came easily, he wasn't worthy of it. These beliefs were not helping his trading. They were actually holding him back!

Now it's time to examine your own money beliefs and where they came from. The following exercises will help you with this process.

EXERCISE #3A:
EXAMINE YOUR MONEY BELIEFS

Write down the beliefs you have about money in the space below. Here's a few examples to get you started:

- "Money doesn't grow on trees."
- "You have to work hard for money."
- "Money Flows Naturally...like water."

EXERCISE #3A:
EXAMINE YOUR MONEY BELIEFS

Please use his page to continue writing answers to Exercise #3A

EXCERISE #3B:
ROOTS OF YOUR MONEY BELIEFS

Now let's dig a little deeper...

Think back to your early childhood. What are 5 things you remember hearing your parents or guardians say about money?

EXCERISE #3C:
ENVIRONMENT PLAYS A ROLE

Your environment influences your beliefs as well.

Think about the 5 people that are closest to you right now. Write their names and add some of the things you've heard them say on the topic of money or finance.

Person 1: ______________________________________

Person 2: ______________________________________

Person 3: ______________________________________

Person 4: ______________________________________

Person 5: ______________________________________

HACK #3: RECAP

You're doing amazing!

In a few short pages you've become immensely more aware of:

1. Why you're trading. How fun it is for you. And why it's important to you.
2. Many of your beliefs about trading.
3. Many of your beliefs about money and the potential influence those closest to you may be having.

You've easily done more mindset work already than the vast majority have. Give yourself another pat on the back!

Next, I want you to get up. Move around. And take a breather!

The exercises coming up are where we start bridging the gap between where you are now and where you ultimately want to be.

HACK #4

Weed Your Mind of Poor Beliefs

Think of your mind as a garden. Like all gardens, it needs weeding from time to time.

You've already gone outside and assessed what's in your mental garden. You've tested the soil. Found some belief plants you like and want to keep. Maybe you found a few weeds too that are preventing you from having the garden of your dreams.

Now it's time to start weeding!

How do you do it? Great question!

Begin by thinking of yourself as an acorn capable of growing into a giant tree.

Now understand that most acorns never reach their potential. Most lay on the forest floor. Some get eaten by squirrels. But that's not you.

In your story, a farmer comes along and offers to help you.

"I'll plant you wherever you like" said the farmer. "You could be planted in a nice cozy pot. Live indoors, sheltered from the elements and live comfortably. Or be planted in the forest and given the opportunity to reach your full potential."

Which do you choose and why?

How you answer depends on your goal, right? Is your goal to be comfortable or is it to achieve your potential?

If your goal is to become a giant tree, you're not picking the cozy pot are you? You need to grow deep roots. To do that, you need to push through dirt and rock. None of this is comfortable. It requires work. But this is what it takes to achieve your potential.

Thankfully, *you* are not a tree, and *you* don't live in a pot.

You can choose to step outside of your comfort zone, get uncomfortable, and keep growing!

This is a lesson I learned on my own the hard way. And it took me nearly a DECADE to do it.

EXERCISE #4A:
ARE YOUR BELIEFS HELPING OR HURTING YOU?

Limiting beliefs can really mess up your trading. The sad reality is that most people are completely unaware of this. They just lay there, beaten-up on the trading floor, wondering why they continue to fail. But that's not you. Not after this exercise!

I'd like you to take out the goals you wrote earlier in Exercise 1B. Keep those next to you.

Next take out the beliefs you wrote about trading and about money in Exercises 2 and 3.

To keep with our gardening analogy, your goals help you figure out what kind of tree you want to grow into and where you want to be planted. Your beliefs are the soil, water, and sunlight to help you grow.

Now let's get them all aligned.

EXERCISE #4A:
ARE YOUR BELIEFS HELPING OR HURTING YOU?

You've got a lot of writing ahead. For this part, grab a separate pad of paper, or start writing in the following pages.

Here's what you're going to do. Rewrite your goals at the top of the page. Then go through each belief you wrote down previously and ask the following questions:

1. Is this belief helping me achieve my goal?
2. Is this belief serving me in some other way right now? If yes, in what ways?
3. How has this belief been useful to me in the past?
4. What did this belief get me into?
5. What did it get me out of?
6. Where did this belief come from?
7. If this belief isn't serving me now, can I let it go? *(If yes, kiss it goodbye! If not, ask yourself why and highlight the belief. Circle it, put a star next to it, etc… We'll come back to it.)*

Go ahead. Do this exercise Now!

EXERCISE #4A:
ARE YOUR BELIEFS HELPING OR HURTING YOU?

EXERCISE #4A:
ARE YOUR BELIEFS HELPING
OR HURTING YOU?

HACK #4: RECAP

Well done! You're crushing it! Seriously!

You're increasingly aware of your beliefs. How they're serving you. Whether or not they are leading you closer to your goals. And where they came from!

You've embraced the beliefs that are leading you closer to your goals. You were even able to start letting go of some of the beliefs that are no longer serving you.

This deserves a double pat on the back and a high five!

By now you know the drill. Time to get up. Move around. Take another breather!

Next, we're going to take a deeper look at those limiting beliefs you highlighted that aren't serving you but you've had some trouble letting go of.

HACK #5

Cutting the
"Limiting Beliefs" Cord

There is a legend of the Gordian Knot.

In 333 B.C., a young Alexander the Great came across a wagon. Its yoke was tied with several knots so entangled that it was impossible to see how they were fastened.

An oracle had prophesized that any man who could unravel its intricate knots was destined to become ruler of all of Asia.

Seized with a desire to untangle the knot, Alexander wrestled with it for a time but unsuccessfully.

He stepped back and exclaimed, "It makes no difference how they are loosed." He then drew his sword and sliced the knot in half with a single stroke.

In another version of the legend, he simply pulled out a lynchpin, loosening the knot enough that he was able to unfasten it.

Whichever way he did it, Alexander outsmarted the ancient riddle, and went on to conquer Egypt and large parts of Asia.

Today, the saying "cutting the Gordian knot" is commonly used to describe a creative or decisive solution to a seemingly insurmountable problem.

Imagine you are like young Alexander, unraveling a cord and all of a sudden you find a big knot. Before you can move forward, you have to deal with the knot.

Maybe you can slice it in half, or maybe you need to detect the "lynchpin." Once you pull out the lynchpin to your problem, you can unravel the rest of the knot.

You've gained awareness of some of your own knots. Choose to leave them alone and you'll find that it trips you up at the worst possible times. It's unavoidable until, like Alexander, you find a way to deal with it. Once you deal with the knot then things can move forward smoothly again. If another knot appears, you deal with that one too.

In Section 4 of this workbook, we touched upon limiting beliefs that weren't serving us. You were able to let go of some of your limiting beliefs quite easily. However, others were like that Gordian Knot. You can't find the lynchpin…or you don't want to cut it out of your life.

Now we need to uncover…Why?

If you are having trouble letting go of a belief that isn't serving you, ask yourself why. Whatever the answer is, it represents another belief and perhaps… the lynchpin.

The following exercise will help you step into the deep end of the pool. But you're not stepping in without a life jacket. You have the tools you need to swim. And trust me, I know how difficult it can be.

As deep as we've gone together in this workbook, this is still just the beginning of your journey. As you grow and evolve, there will be new challenges and new knots to face. Unlike most people who are unaware or pretend these knots don't exist, you are taking real action today! You're not only facing these knots, but like Alexander, you're doing something about it!

This is true life changing work you are doing. When you answer the following questions, be honest with yourself and answer the questions truthfully. The only person you'll be hurting by not being honest with yourself is YOU.

EXERCISE #5:
CUT THE "LIMITING BELIEFS" CORD

For every belief that you highlighted in Section Four, re-write them on the following pages (or separate sheets of paper). Then ask the following questions of each belief:

1.   Where did this belief come from?
2.   What stage of life was I in when I acquired this belief?
3.   What other belief(s) is this belief tied to?
4.   What would happen if I let this belief go?
5.   What will happen if I continue to hold this belief?
6.   How will my life and trading look in the next 6 months if I continue holding this belief?
7.   How about the next year?
8.   What if I continue holding this belief for another 5, 10, or even 20 years?
9.   Now ask yourself, 'Given the above answers, am I really willing to continue holding this belief?'

EXERCISE #5:
CUT THE "LIMITING BELIEFS" CORD

EXERCISE #5:
CUT THE "LIMITING BELIEFS" CORD

HACK #5: RECAP

Now that you've weeded your mental garden, plant only the beliefs that serve you and move you closer to your goals.

You can let go of old beliefs that are limiting you. You can change your beliefs. You can improve your beliefs. You can even adopt new beliefs! Beliefs that align with your goals and bring you closer to everything you hope to achieve!

Remember, nothing is permanent. If you want your mental garden to flourish, it'll take some maintenance. Start by setting up time to meet with coaches and mentors that can help you grow. If you'd like me to be your coach, go to marawealth.com, click the 'membership' tab, and sign up.

Review your beliefs regularly. Aim for once a month to start. With the mental renovation you've already done, monthly maintenance will be easy.

Yes, it will take some effort. But much like the tree which grows in the forest, your potential lies in the challenges you are willing to face.

NEXT STEPS FOR TRADING SUCCESS

Now that you've weeded your mental garden, your next step is to plant some new beliefs. Beliefs that will begin serving you immediately and will continue to serve you on your journey toward your trading goals.

These new beliefs can be broken down into 8 categories. I call them the '8 Core Skills of Trading Mastery.'

THE 8 CORE SKILLS OF TRADING MASTERY

There are 8 skills that you'll need to include in your mental garden, no matter what kind of trader you hope to become. Day trader, swing trader, long term investor. It doesn't matter. These 8 core skills will propel you toward consistent profitability, trading mastery, and achieving all of your other trading goals.

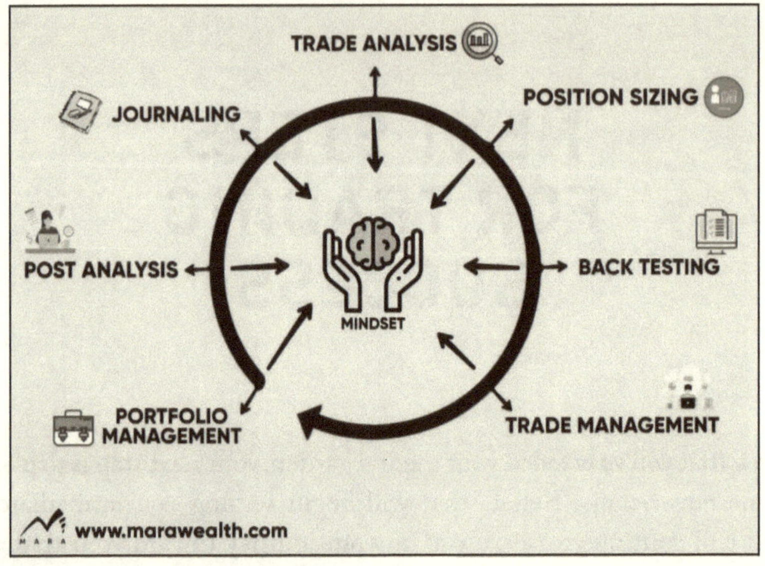

1. Trade Analysis: 'Trade Analysis' is both analysis of the individual trade you're considering, as well as an analysis of the market environment you're considering taking it in.

How will you gauge market direction or what I call the 'Market's Mood'? How will you determine if it is trending up, down, or sideways? If it is volatile or quiet? If the conditions are right for your trading style or not?

For the individual trades, what separates a 'good setup' from a 'great one'?

You must clearly define under what circumstances you'll enter the trade, take profits, and cut your losses.

2. Position Sizing: How much will you risk on each trade? This is what your position sizing strategy answers. While there are many ways to answer this, YOUR ANSWER will depend on YOUR GOALS.

If part of your goal is to stay in the game for as long as possible, not risk too much per trade, and keep your risk levels consistent (same dollar amount risked per trade), I've created a tool that will help you. It's position size calculator that you can use for free. Go to www.marawealth.com and have a look.

3. Trade Management: Your trade management strategy looks at any trades you have open and helps you determine where you'll exit (with a profit or a loss), where you'll add, and how much for each.

To help you get started, here are some of the basics of my personal trade management strategy and philosophy.

I view trades similar to how you'd watch a movie in a theater.

First, the movie has to be something you feel is worth your time and money. If it is, you buy your tickets and head into the theater.

Before you sit down, it's good to know where all the exits are, right?

Often the first and closest exit is right behind you. If the movie stinks after the first 20 minutes, you can always cut your losses, save an hour or two, and walk out the back. This is akin to the stop loss of a trade.

But theaters have more than one exit. You'll often find exits on the left, right, and even in the front by the screen. Just like theaters have multiple exits planned, we should plan multiple exits for our trades.

In addition to the stop loss, I use a series of profit targets, trailing stops, and backstops as exits for my trades.

4. Portfolio Management: Your portfolio management strategy answers the questions, "how many?" and "how much total?"

How many positions will you have open at any one time?

How much of your total capital will be at risk at any one time? For example, if you risk 1% of capital per trade and start five new positions, you'd be risking 5% total.

No matter how many trades you plan on taking, a question worth asking yourself is, "what would happen if my stop loss hits on all of them?"

5. Back testing: How do you know if your strategy works? How do you do this BEFORE putting money at risk?? The answer, back testing.

There are lots of ways to back test and plenty of software available to help with the task. The best way I know to do it is to start with the following:

a. Gain clarity on your goals (you did that already!)
b. Research strategies and styles that will help you meet those goals. They're out there. You don't need to reinvent the wheel.
c. Once you've found some styles you like, start testing! You'll need a minimum of 100 trades to gain statistical significance and see if the strategy REALLY works.

6. Journaling: After going through this Mindshift Guide, you've likely gained an appreciation for how powerful writing can be for you. Well, this too is just the beginning!

A well-thought-out trade journal is a key tool in every great trader's arsenal. This is where you keep track of your trades, analysis, position sizing, trade management, portfolio management, and other trade-related thoughts (including your mental state).

Similar to back testing, there are plenty of ways to journal. My first journals consisted of binders where I'd print charts, write notes on them, and parse them by winning and losing trades.

The key to journaling is to simply get started. To help get you started, I've created a simple journaling template called the 'Trade Tracker'. You can download it free at www.marawealth.com.

7. Post Analysis: Continuous improvement in your trading happens not just from tracking your trades in a journal, but from reviewing those trades. What went well? What didn't? What can be improved?

Set a schedule for how often you'll do this and stick to it.

If you want to achieve mastery faster, I recommend a light review of your trades at the end of each trading day after the market has closed. Ask yourself:

a. Did you stick to your trading plan?
b. Did you follow your entry and exit strategies?
c. Did you follow your trade management, portfolio management, and position sizing strategies?
d. How can you improve tomorrow?

At the end of each week, take an overall assessment. This will help you figure out where you need to improve and begin to develop strategies on how to do it.

At the end of the month, take account of everything that happened during that month. What worked? What didn't? Has your lifestyle changed? How may it impact your trading? What, if anything, must change to stay on course to hit your goals?

8. Mindset: Mindset is the lynchpin of the other 7 core skills and is a skill unto itself. You've taken great strides in improving your mindset by completing the exercises in this workbook and learning about the 8 core skills you need to achieve trading mastery.

Mindset is at the core and holds everything together. Van Tharp, another market wizard, famously said, "We don't actually trade the market. We trade our beliefs about the market." After completing the exercises in this workbook, you know that this is the case.

Now, I have just one more exercise for you in this Mindshift Guide. This one will help you assess your strengths and weaknesses and where you'll need to focus your efforts next.

EXERCISE:
8 CORE TRADING SKILLS SCORECARD

Give yourself a score of 1 to 5 on the following 8 Core Trading Skills. A "1" is low, and a "5" is high. The goal isn't to be perfect; it's to become more self-aware.

8 CORE TRADING SKILLS CHART

TRADE ANALYSIS	
POSITION SIZING	
TRADE MANAGEMENT	
PORTFOLIO MANAGEMENT	
BACK TESTING	
JOURNALING	
POST ANALYSIS	
MINDSET	

YOUR NEXT STEP!

Now that you have rated yourself on each of the 8 Core Trading Skills, your next step is to develop a game plan for improving the areas you scored lowest in.

I started MARA Wealth to help traders like you succeed in the market and avoid the many pitfalls I made when I started trading over 20 years ago. Back then, I had no idea that there are 8 trading skills I needed to master…and I struggled alone for nearly a decade!

I want to let you know that there is an easier way to learn and master all of these 8 core skills than doing it on your own.

Every day our MARA Elite members are drilling these skills. Every day we're discussing them in our forums, sharing ideas, and supporting one another.

Every weekend we're meeting virtually on Zoom together, analyzing markets, identifying trades, skillfully, and objectively assessing whether ideas are worth the risk.

We game plan together, back test together, and have special focused monthly Boot Camps together.

We'd love to have you as part of our Elite team! Check out marawealth. com/membership/ and use Coupon Code "MARABeliefs10" to get 10%-Off your 6-month subscription if you sign up today!

You will be working with me in our Live Group Coaching sessions. I'll help you plant even better trading beliefs and develop stronger trading habits.

Remember, you do not trade the market. You trade your beliefs about the market. So it's best if you continued to care for your mental garden. Add these 8 core skills and watch your trading garden flourish far beyond your wildest dreams!

FINAL THOUGHT

CONGRATS!!

You succeeded in completing the MARA Mindshift Guide! This isn't the end. It's a new beginning.

After reading this book and doing the exercises, you now have better awareness of your goals, trading beliefs, money beliefs and what you are striving for.

I've run a few marathons in my life, and I've done it with teams, and being able to do it with a team just makes it so much easier. I've also seen people run marathons that are blind, that have only prosthetic legs, that are wheelchair bound and pushing themselves backwards in their wheelchair for 26.2 miles just to complete it.

Anyone determined enough can complete a marathon. Anyone determined enough can create wealth. You find a way to make it happen.

With the completion of this workbook, you have a solid game plan. Now it's a matter of continuing to take action on all the things we've spoken about already.

We don't need to do these things alone. In fact, when we're doing these things together as a group, it not only makes it so much easier, it makes it fun. Trading is, and wealth creation is a journey. It's a marathon. It's challenging. And with enough determination, it's something that is attainable by anyone.

Thank you so much for taking action today and for completing the MARA Mindshift Guide. You've come a LONG way in just a few short pages. There's so much promise for you in the market, in trading, and in life! I'm so glad to be a part of your journey.

If I can personally help you with anything, please feel free to reach out. You can reach me on http://www.marawealth.com and follow me on Instagram/Stocktwits/Twitter **@michaelglamothe**.

ACKNOWLEDGMENTS

There are many people I'd like to acknowledge in writing this workbook and without whom the final product would not have been possible.

To my wife, editor, and writing coach Melissa. What an incredible journey this has been! What we started originally as a 5 page blog post now turned into a nearly 70 page life changing workbook. It blows my mind! Thank you for being there with me through it all and helping to bring this to life. I love you.

To my daughter Lily. You are a constant source of inspiration.

To all of our beta readers including Rizwan Memon, Jason Graystone, Akil Stokes, Austin Silver, Christopher Uhl, Rolf Scholotmann, Tyler Dupont, Jim Roppel, Erik Smolinski, Pierce Crosby, Larry Tentarelli, Patrick Walker, Mike Webster, Alex Bustos, Kevin Marder, Kevin Cook, Mark Minervini, Felix Frey, and Adam Sarhan, you helped in so many ways. From words of encouragement, to minor tweaks, to major additions. Thank you!

And to our interior designer and book cover designer Richell, thank you for making this look and feel as awesome as it does.

ABOUT THE AUTHOR

Michael Lamothe has 20+ years of research and trading experience. After years of encountering obstacles, Michael came up with a solution to help part-time and full-time traders succeed in the market. He founded MARA Wealth in 2018, and his mission is to help traders succeed in the market, with a focus on the 8 core trading skills to achieve trading mastery, with emphasis on mindset  and trading beliefs. Michael has helped thousands of traders through his methodology and has been called one of the TOP Trading Mindset Coaches in the US. He is an international speaker, presenting at AAII, Thought Leadership Academy, and Stocktoberfest, and has been featured on Nasdaq Live. For additional information, please go to www.Marawealth.com. Follow Michael on Instagram, Stocktwits, and Twitter: @MichaelGLamothe.